D1261968

Let's Explore
Comets
and
Asteroids

Helen and David Orme

GARETH**STEVENS**
PUBLISHING
A Member of the WRC Media Family of Companies

Please visit our Web site at: www.garethstevens.com
For a free color catalog describing Gareth Stevens Publishing's list
of high-quality books and multimedia programs, call
1-800-542-2595 (USA) or 1-800-387-3178 (Canada).
Gareth Stevens Publishing's fax: (414) 332-3567.

Library of Congress Cataloging-in-Publication Data

Orme, Helen.
    Let's explore comets and asteroids / Helen and David Orme.
       p. cm. — (Space launch!)
    Includes index.
    ISBN-13: 978-0-8368-7947-6 (lib. bdg.)
    ISBN-13: 978-0-8368-8132-5 (softcover)
    1. Comets—Juvenile literature. 2. Asteroids—Juvenile literature.
  I. Orme, David, 1948 Mar. 1- II. Title.
  QB721.5.O76 2007
  523.44—dc22   2006034715

This North American edition first published in 2007 by
Gareth Stevens Publishing
A Member of the WRC Media Family of Companies
330 West Olive Street, Suite 100
Milwaukee, Wisconsin 53212 USA

This U.S. edition copyright © 2007 by Gareth Stevens, Inc. Original edition copyright © 2006 by ticktock Entertainment
Ltd. First published in Great Britain in 2006 by ticktock Media Ltd., Unit 2, Orchard Business Centre, North Farm Road,
Tunbridge Wells, Kent, TN2 3XF, United Kingdom.

The publishers would like to thank: Sandra Voss, Tim Bones, James Powell, Indexing Specialists (UK) Ltd.

ticktock project editor: Julia Adams
ticktock project designer: Emma Randall

Gareth Stevens Editorial Direction: Mark Sachner
Gareth Stevens Editors: Barbara Kiely Miller and Carol Ryback
Gareth Stevens Art Direction: Tammy West
Gareth Stevens Designer: Dave Kowalski
Gareth Stevens Production: Jessica Yanke and Robert Kraus

Photo credits (t=top, b=bottom, c=center, l=left, r=right, bg=background)
Brigdeman: 17t; CORBIS: 20; NASA: 7tr, 7cl, 7c, 7bl, 10, 11, 17b, 22, 23t; Science Photo Libary: 4/5bg (original), 8, 14, 15t; Shutterstock: 2/3bg,
6, 7cr, 9t, 24bg; ticktock image library: front cover, 1 all, 5tr, 6/7bg, 9b, 10/11bg, 12, 13, 14/15bg, 15br, 15bl, 16, 18/19bg, 18, 19, 21, 22/23bg, 23.
Rocket drawing Dave Kowalski/ Gareth Stevens, Inc.

Every effort has been made to trace the copyright holders for the photos used in this book. The publisher apologizes,
in advance, for any unintentional omissions and would be pleased to insert the appropriate acknowledgments in
any subsequent edition of this publication.

All rights reserved. No part of this book may be reproduced, stored in a retrieval system, or transmitted
in any form or by any means, electronic, mechanical, photocopying, recording, or otherwise, without the
prior written permission of the publisher.

Printed in Canada

1 2 3 4 5 6 7 8 9 10 10 09 08 07 06

Contents

Words in the glossary are printed in **bold** the first time they appear in the text.

The Solar System

The **solar system** includes the Sun, planets, and moons. Thousands of smaller objects, called **comets** and **asteroids**, also **orbit** the Sun.

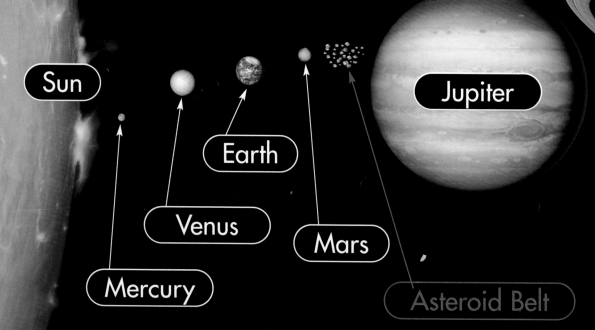

Sun

Mercury

Venus

Earth

Mars

Jupiter

Asteroid Belt

The solar system formed billions of years ago from a spinning disk of gas and dust. Most of the material in the disk became the Sun.

Some of the material formed planets and moons. The rest of the material formed comets and asteroids.

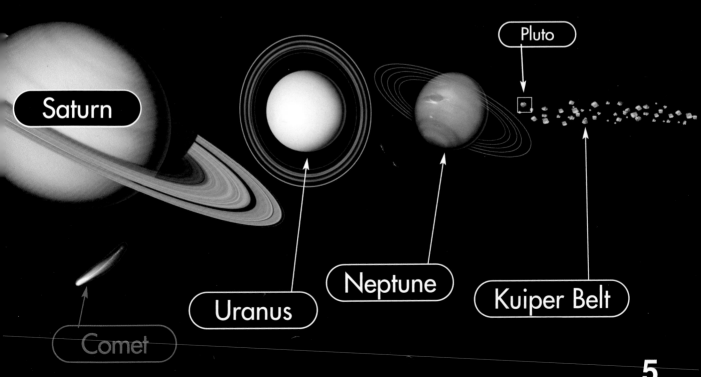

Pluto

Saturn

Uranus

Neptune

Kuiper Belt

Comet

What Is an Asteroid?

An asteroid is a big space rock. Most asteroids measure less than 1 mile (1.6 kilometers) across.

asteroids

Ceres is large object between Mars and Jupiter. **Astronomers** used to call Ceres a large asteroid.

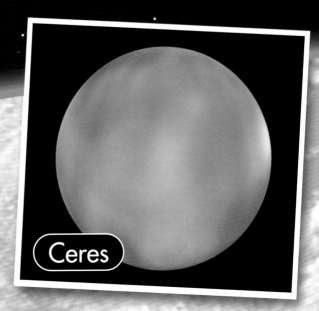
Ceres

In 2006, astronomers decided that Ceres is really a **dwarf planet** instead of an asteroid. The pictures below show the sizes of Ceres, the Moon, and Earth.

Ceres
620 miles
(998 km)

2,160 miles
(3,476 km)
Moon

7,926 miles
(12,757 km)
Earth

Most asteroids are not round like Ceres. They can have any shape, like this bumpy asteroid.

7

Where are Asteroids?

Like the planets and Ceres, asteroids orbit the Sun. Most asteroids that we know about are found in an **asteroid belt** between Mars and Jupiter.

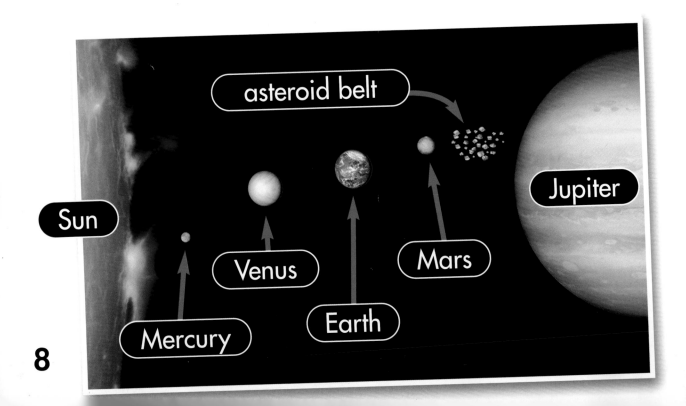

Sun

Mercury

Venus

Earth

Mars

asteroid belt

Jupiter

shooting star

Objects called **meteoroids**, which are space rocks smaller than asteroids, sometimes hit Earth's **atmosphere**. Meteoroids burn up in bright flashes of light called **meteors**, or **shooting stars**.

Meteors that do not burn up completely and reach the ground are called **meteorites**. This meteorite was found in Los Angeles, California, in October 1999.

1.5 inches
(3.8 centimeters)

Hunting for Asteroids

Astronomers are always looking for new asteroids. Every month, they find thousands more!

Mathilde

Eros

the asteroids Mathilde and Eros

Some asteroids are named for the people who discovered them. Others are named after famous people. One asteroid is named "Rowling" to honor the author of the *Harry Potter* books!

Astronomers keep track of thousands of asteroids that orbit near Earth.

Earth

asteroid

The asteroid in this drawing looks like it is very close to Earth. In fact, it is many thousands of miles away!

Astronomers think a huge asteroid hit Earth millions of years ago. They believe the asteroid changed Earth so much that all the dinosaurs died!

asteroid

Earth

What is a Comet?

A comet is a space object that travels through the solar system in a wide orbit. We only see comets when their orbit passes near the Sun.

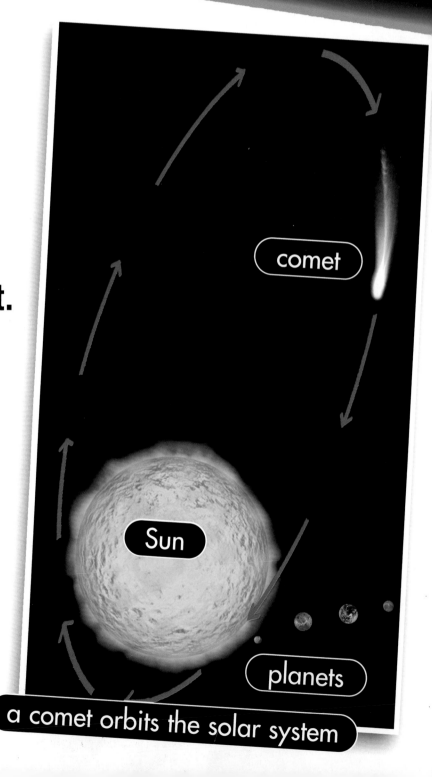

comet

Sun

planets

a comet orbits the solar system

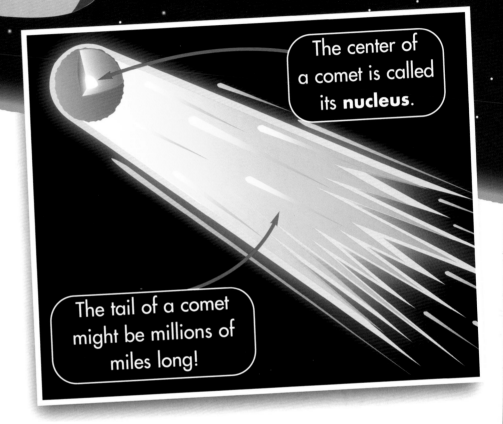

The center of a comet is called its **nucleus**.

The tail of a comet might be millions of miles long!

Comets are a mixture of dust and ice. Some of them may have a rocky center.

Heat from the Sun burns up dust and gases in the comet as it nears the Sun. The burning materials form a bright "tail" that points away from the Sun.

Comet Hale-Bopp has two tails. One tail is made of gases. The brighter tail is made of dust and ice that shines in the sunlight.

gas tail

dust tail

13

Where are Comets?

Astronomers think most comets come from an area far out in space called the **Oort Cloud**. The Oort Cloud is found at the outer edge of our solar system.

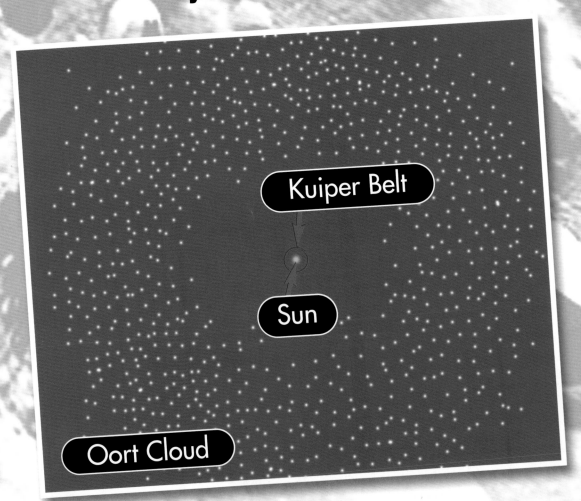

Kuiper Belt

Sun

Oort Cloud

comet

Mercury

Earth's Moon and some planets, such as Mercury, may have ice on them. Comets crashing into these objects may have left the ice behind.

Comet Shoemaker-Levy 9 crashed into Jupiter in 1994. Many comets crash into the Sun instead of into a planet.

Shoemaker-Levy 9

Jupiter

Shoemaker-Levy 9

Comets and Earth

Ancient people did not understand that comets were simply big, dusty ice balls. They believed a comet was a sign that something bad would happen.

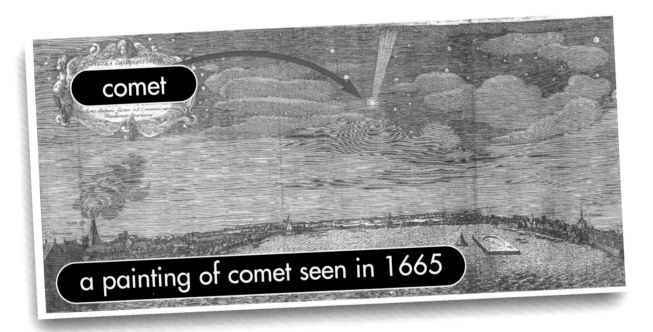

comet

a painting of comet seen in 1665

For a long time, people thought comets caused problems such as wars, sickness, and bad weather.

This drawing from 1759 shows people studying a comet with a **telescope**.

comet

comet

a drawing of a comet hitting Earth

Now we know that comets are not warnings from space. Astronomers think that comets hitting Earth millions of years ago left behind ice and dust that may have helped life begin to form.

What Can We See?

From Earth, a comet looks like a bright, fuzzy blob with one or two tails.

Vesta

Unlike comets, asteroids are much harder to see. Only one asteroid, called Vesta, can be seen from Earth without a telescope.

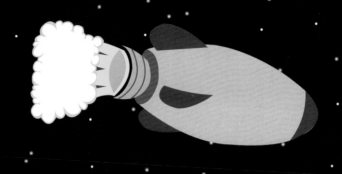

Halley's comet

Halley's comet comes closer to Earth about every 76 years. You will have to wait until July 2061 to see Halley's comet!

In 1066, the French saw a comet before a big battle with the English. They sewed a picture history of the battle, called the **Bayeux tapestry**. It shows what we call Halley's comet in the sky.

comet

Early Sightings

Early astronomers had no idea what comets or asteroids were. To them, comets and asteroids were special bright lights in the night sky.

This picture shows an astronomer studying the sky hundreds of years ago.

English astronomer Edmond Halley lived from 1656 to 1742. In 1705, he figured out that comets follow a set orbit through the solar system. The comet that he said would appear in 1758 and about every 76 years after that is now called Halley's comet.

Italian astronomer Giuseppe Piazzi was the first person to discover an asteroid. In 1801, he found Ceres, which we now call a dwarf planet.

21

Space Missions

In 1999, the *Stardust* mission was launched. *Stardust* was a **space probe** that collected dust from a comet named Wild-2. In early 2006, *Stardust* returned to Earth.

Stardust space probe

comet Wild-2

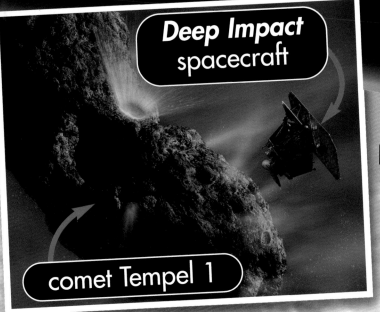

Deep Impact spacecraft

comet Tempel 1

Hayabusa

Itokawa

In July 2005, the *Deep Impact* mission crashed a small space probe into comet Tempel 1. The crash made a dent, or **crater**, on Tempel 1. The *Deep Impact* spacecraft then studied the layers of dirt, ice, and rocks of the crater.

In 2005, the Japanese space probe *Hayabusa* made two short landings on the asteroid called Itokawa. Astronomers will not know if *Hayabusa* collected samples until it returns to Earth in 2010.

Glossary

asteroids large rocky objects that orbit the Sun.

asteroid belt an area of space that is full of asteroids. It is located between Mars and Jupiter.

astronomers scientists who study outer space, often using telescopes

atmosphere the gases that surround a planet, moon, or star

Bayeux tapestry a nearly thousand-year-old sewn history that is about 230 feet (70 meters) long. It shows the Battle of Hastings, often called the Norman (or French), conquest of England, fought in 1066.

comets dusty ice balls that follow a wide orbit around the solar system

crater a dent or rounded hole in the surface of a planet or moon

dwarf planet a planet smaller than Mercury

meteoroids space rocks smaller than asteroids found in the solar system

meteorites pieces of space rocks that land on a planet's or moon's surface

meteors (shooting stars) the bright flashes of space dust or rocks burning up in Earth's atmosphere

nucleus the very center of an object

Oort Cloud an area at the farthest edges of the solar system

orbit the path that one space object takes around another space object

shooting stars (meteors) the bright flashes of space dust or rocks burning up in Earth's atmosphere

solar system the Sun and everything that is in orbit around it

space probe a spacecraft sent from Earth to explore the solar system and take pictures

telescope an instrument used for studying objects that are very far away

Index